Learn YOGA by coloring

PLEASANT POSE

SUKHASANA

A comfortable position for the meditation and pranayamas practice

Strengthens concentration

BOUND ANGLE POSE

BADDHA KONASANA

Improves posture

Stretches the inner thighs

Improves circulation

Increases flexibility of the hips

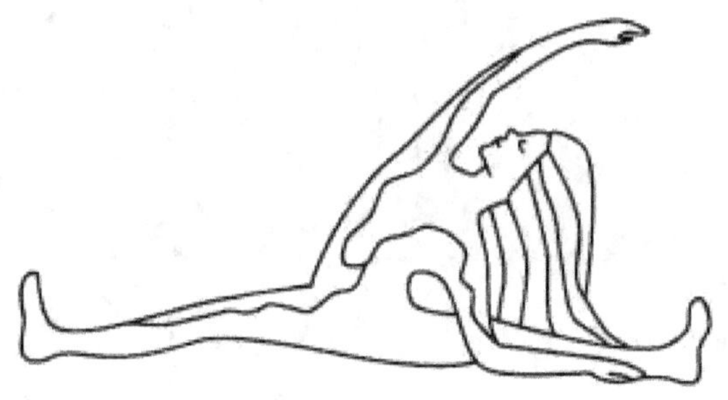

REVOLVED HEAD-TO-KNEE POSE

PARIVRTTA JANU SIRSASANA

Stretches the legs and waist muscles

Frees the tension from the neck and shoulder region

Expands the chest

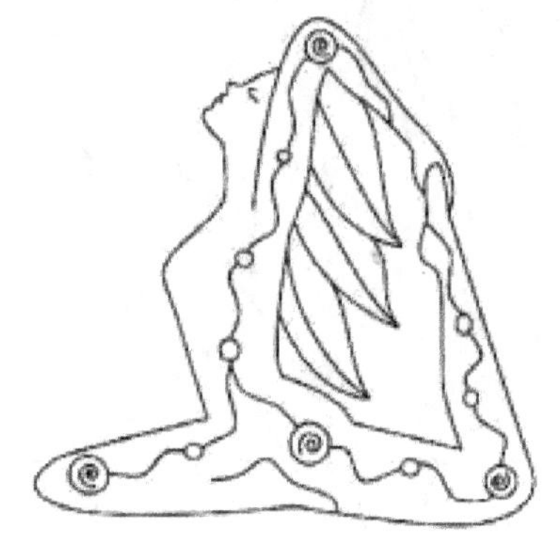

ONE-LEGGED KING PIGEON POSE

EKA PADA RA JAKAPOTASANA

Improves balance

Strengthens the spine

Stretches the lower back and thighs

Expands the chest

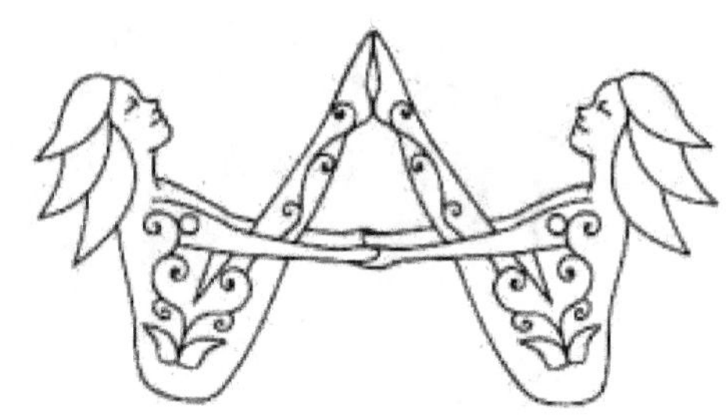

BUDDY BOAT POSE

NAVASANA

Stretches the leg muscles

Helps partners performing the pose to develop mutual trust

BIG TOE POSE

PADANGUSTHASANA

Improves balance and concentration

Stretches and strengthens the leg muscles

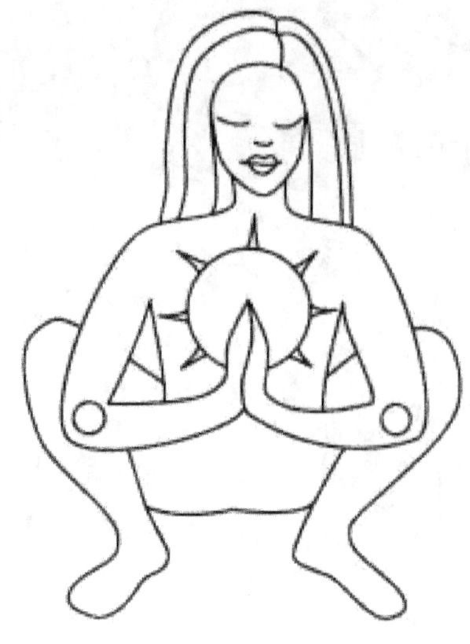

CHAIR POSE

UTKATASANA

Improves concentration

Improves flexibility of the leg joints

Expands the chest

Strengthens the shoulders and the chest

CRANE POSE

BAKASANA

Improves balance and concentration

Strengthens the shoulders, forearms and wrists

Gently stretches the spine

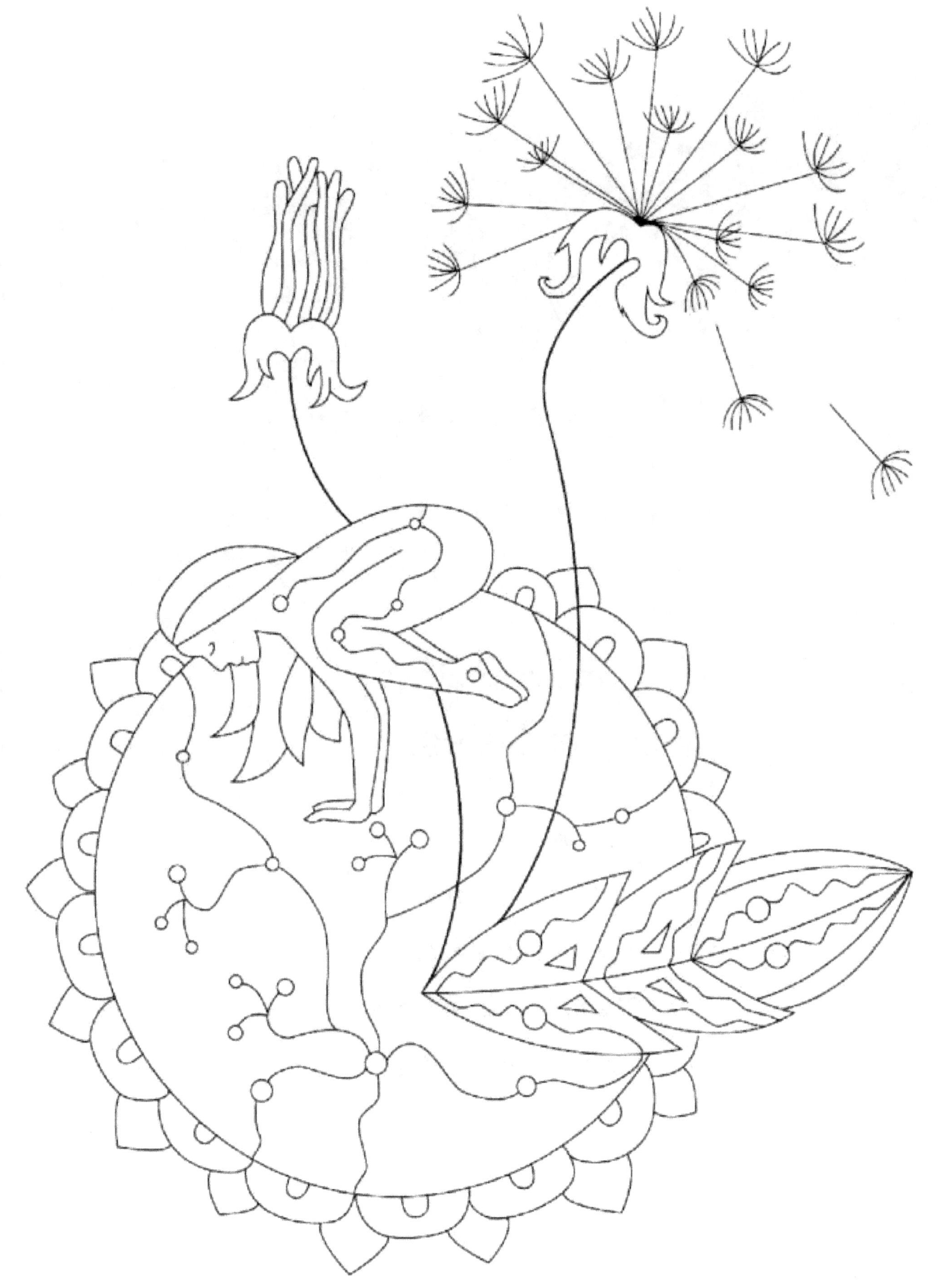

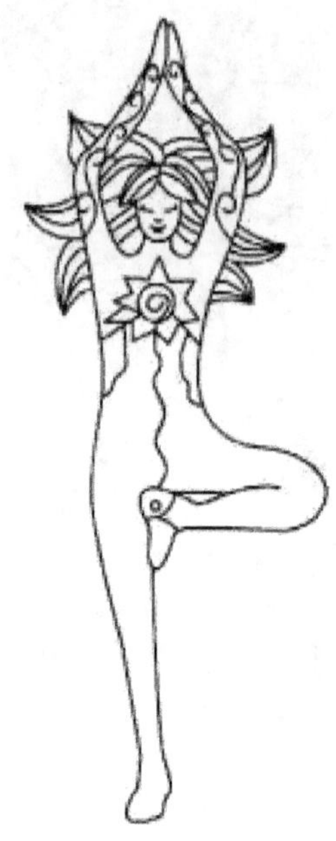

TREE POSE

VRKSASANA

Improves balance

Calms the mind

Boosts concentration

Strengthens the thighs

Stretches the inner thighs

LORD OF THE DANCE POSE

NATARA JASANA

Improves balance and concentration

Expands the chest

Strengthens the muscles of the legs and the hips

Stretches and strengthens the back muscles

TRIANGLE POSE

TRIKONASANA

Improves digestion

Strengthens the legs, knees, arms and chest

Stretches the thighs, hips, calves, shoulders, chest and spine

FIVE POINTED STAR POSE

UTTHITA TADASANA

Improves posture

Expands the chest

BOAT POSE

NAVASANA

Improves digestion

Helps to release the stress

Strengthens the muscles of the abdominal wall

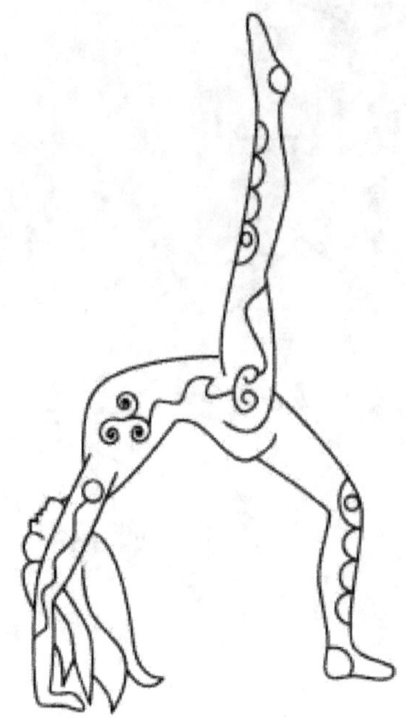

WHEEL POSE

CHAKRASANA

Strenghtens the arms, legs and shoulders

Stretches the chest and abdominal muscles

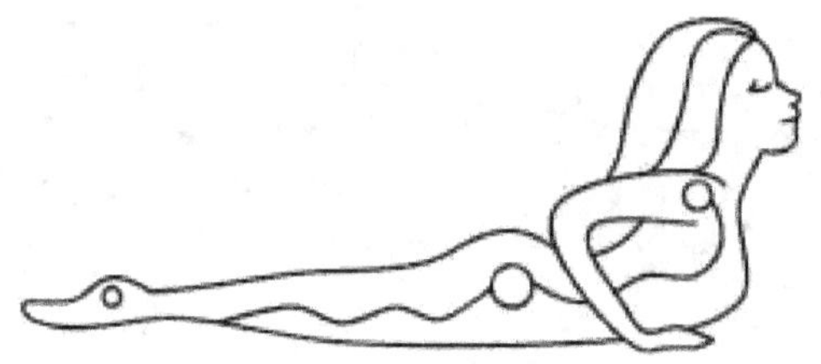

COBRA POSE

BHUJANGASANA

Improves posture

Strengthens the back and neck muscles

Expands the chest

THE HALF SPINAL TWIST POSE

ARDHA MATSYENDRASANA

Increases flexibility of the spine and hips

Stimulates digestion

BOW POSE

DHANURASANA

Increases flexibility of the spine

Strengthens back muscles, thighs and breasts

Improves posture

Gently massages the organs of the abdominal cavity

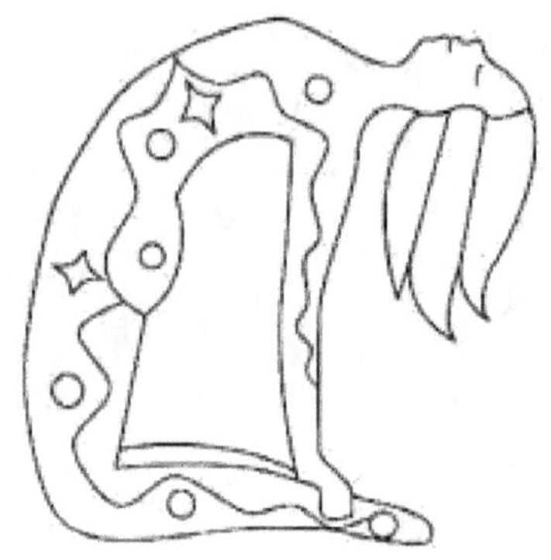

CAMEL POSE

USHTRASANA

Increases the lung capacity

Stimulates the organs of the abdominal cavity

Strengthens the back muscles

Stretches the stomach muscles

Improves digestion

Text, cover pages and drawings:
Dušanka Milovanović, certified yoga instructor
Tijana Cosic

Review:
Jovana Marinkovic

The publisher:
Jovana Marinkovic

Press:
Belpak, Belgrade

Copy:
100

Belgrade, 2016

ISBN 978-86-920843-0-0